A Girlfriend's Handbook

Dating a
LIAR,
a
CHEATER,

and a
JERK

100 Reasons Why You
Should Take Him Back

KIM WIEDERHOLT

ISBN: 1-4196-8095-1
ISBN-13: 978-1-4196-8095-3

CONTENTS

Preface...v

Chapter One: Simply Put.........1

PREFACE

As women,

we deserve respect and adoration.
So why take him back when he is
dishonest, unfaithful and thoughtless?
The reasons...

CHAPTER ONE

Simply Put...

www.ingramcontent.com/pod-product-compliance
Lightning Source LLC
Chambersburg PA
CBHW060419290526
45791CB00002B/820